WHAT EVERY TE

MW01613201

Theology

Developed by the
Christian Education Staff
of The General Board of Discipleship
of The United Methodist Church

DISCIPLESHIP RESOURCES

P.O. BOX 340003 • NASHVILLE, TN 37203-0003
www.discipleshipresources.org

This booklet was developed by the Christian Education Staff of The General Board of Discipleship of The United Methodist Church. It is one in a series of booklets designed to provide essential knowledge for teachers. Members of the staff who helped write and develop this series are Terry Carty, Bill Crenshaw, Donna Gaither, Rick Gentzler, Mary Alice Gran, Susan Hay, Betsey Heavner, Diana Hynson, Carol Krau, MaryJane Pierce Norton, Deb Smith, Julia Wallace, and Linda Whited.

Cover and book design by Joey McNair
Cover illustration by Mike Drake

Edited by Debra D. Smith and Cindy S. Harris

ISBN 0-88177-367-0

DR367

Contents

*This book is dedicated to
YOU,
a teacher of
children, youth, or adults,
WHO,
with fear, excitement, joy,
and commitment,
allows God to lead you
in the call to
TEACH.*

*The gifts he gave were that some would be . . .
teachers, . . . for building up the body of Christ.
(Ephesians 4:11-12)*

Introduction

Teachers and small-group leaders are spiritual
leaders who pay attention to their relationship
with God and others and who seek to live their
faith in their daily lives. They have knowledge and skills
to create safe, healthy settings for people to seek God,
respond to God's grace, and find support and encouragement for living as disciples in the world.

Becoming a spiritual leader is a transformational
experience, which is the work of God. The work of the
congregation is to support teachers and group leaders
by providing opportunities for spiritual growth, opportunities for ongoing learning, resources, and other
materials needed to be effective.

Every sentence of the two preceding paragraphs
describes the role of teachers and small-group leaders.
Each sentence also makes interpretive statements about

teachers: Teachers are spiritual leaders. Teachers value their relationships with God and other people. Teachers experience God's transforming presence through the ministry of teaching and learning. We could spend a lifetime thinking and talking about what it means to be a spiritual leader, how we are transformed by God, and what it means to describe teaching as ministry. The church word we use to describe this kind of reflection and conversation is *theology*.

As a teacher of children, youth, or adults, you select, adapt, and/or write curriculum resources. You choose which learning activities to use with your group. You decide which teaching methods to employ. You build relationships with class members. You consider yourself to be the group's facilitator, or mentor, or teacher, or coach, or friend, or all of the above.

Each of these decisions and choices reflects a particular theological understanding of what your purpose is, of who you are in relationship to God, and of how you view your class members. To a certain extent, someone other than you has determined these theological understandings. If you have purchased curriculum resources, the writers and editors have shaped the material from a particular theological viewpoint. However, the way you use the curriculum resources and design the learning environment reflects *your* theological viewpoint, consciously or unconsciously.

Each of these decisions and choices also has an impact on your class members' theology. What you teach and how you teach can reinforce or contradict learners' own understandings of self, God, the church, and so forth. Our life as a faith community shapes and is shaped by our theology.

This booklet is designed to provide basic information about theology. Depending upon your background, this booklet may serve as a crash course in theology, a reminder of things you have forgotten, or encouragement to explore these topics in more depth.

This booklet is one of ten that will equip you for teaching. Use the entire series to reinforce your own knowledge, skills, and abilities.

Other booklets in this series are
What Every Teacher Needs to Know About
• *the Bible*
• *Christian Heritage*
• *Classroom Environment*
• *Curriculum*
• *Faith Language*
• *Living the Faith*
• *People*
• *Teaching*
• *The United Methodist Church*

So, What Is Theology?

Me? *Know about theology? Forget-about-it.* That may have been your reaction when you read the title of this booklet. If so, you're not alone. The very word *theology* can transform the most confident teacher into a cowering mass of gelatin. Not to worry. It's not nearly as hard to be a theologian as you might think. As a matter of fact, you already are one. Okay, stop laughing. I mean it. As a Christian you are already a theologian.

Defining Theology

In simple terms, *theology* means the study of God (*theos*). The way we think about God, how we talk about God, and what we believe about God make up our theology. We can use complex language to express our theology. For example, in the Christian church, theology also includes what we believe about who Jesus is and how we understand Jesus' life, ministry, death, and resurrection (Christology). Theology also explores the nature of the church (ecclesiology). But all these big words mean is how we think about important "stuff" and what significance and meaning we attach to it.

Each of us has a theology. We may not spend much time consciously thinking about our beliefs. We may not feel comfortable talking about what we believe. But we do have beliefs, values, and assumptions that have been shaped since our childhood. We respond to the world through the lens of these beliefs, values, and assumptions.

Hungering for Truth

The Book of Discipline of The United Methodist Church—2000 states: "To be persons of faith is to hunger to understand the truth given to us in Jesus Christ." (Copyright © 2000 by The United Methodist Publishing House. Used by permission; ¶ 104, page 75.) What a powerful image! Persons of faith are hungry to know God through Jesus Christ. We are ravenous. We want to be satisfied. We can't get enough of God in Christ!

We know that there is great diversity in theological understandings of God, of faith, and of Christian discipleship. This diversity has existed since the church began. Take a look at Acts for some of the arguments about whether or not Gentiles had to be circumcised and follow the Jewish law in order to be Christian. These arguments were not philosophical debates; they were grounded in the theological viewpoints of the various members of the emerging Christian faith. The outcome of the dispute was important to each person involved.

We can easily be swept up in theological debates over issues in today's church. We are called as individuals and as faith communities to engage in serious study, reflection, and prayer as we clarify, test, and renew our interpretation of the gospel for today's context. Our deep yearning for God sustains our efforts.

What are some of the questions of faith that are facing the church today? As you think about those issues, what knowledge and experience have the greatest impact on what you believe about the issues? Write your thoughts in the space below and on the next page.

What Does the Church Believe?

As stated above, there are many different expressions of theology. However, throughout the centuries the Christian church has attempted to describe the basic doctrines of our faith. Here is a brief description of these basics.

Trinity

- We describe God in three persons. Father, Son, and Holy Spirit are commonly used to refer to the three-fold nature of God. Sometimes we use other terms, such as Creator, Redeemer, and Sustainer.

God

- We believe in one God, who created the world and all that is in it.
- We believe that God is sovereign; that is, God is the ruler of the universe.
- We believe that God is loving. We can experience God's love and grace.

Jesus

- We believe that Jesus was human. He lived as a man and died when he was crucified.
- We believe that Jesus is divine. He is the Son of God.
- We believe that God raised Jesus from the dead and that the risen Christ lives today. (*Christ* and *messiah* mean the same thing—God's anointed.)

- We believe that Jesus is our Savior. In Christ we receive abundant life and forgiveness of sins.
- We believe that Jesus is our Lord and that we are called to pattern our lives after his.

The Holy Spirit
- We believe that the Holy Spirit is God with us.
- We believe that the Holy Spirit comforts us when we are in need and convicts us when we stray from God.
- We believe that the Holy Spirit awakens us to God's will and empowers us to live obediently.

Human Beings
- We believe that God created human beings in God's image.
- We believe that humans can choose to accept or reject a relationship with God.
- We believe that all humans need to be in relationship with God in order to be fully human.

The Church
- We believe that the church is the body of Christ, an extension of Christ's life and ministry in the world today.
- We believe that the mission of the church is to make disciples of Jesus Christ.
- We believe that the church is "the communion of saints," a community made up of all past, present, and future disciples of Christ.

- We believe that the church is called to worship God and to support those who participate in its life as they grow in faith.

The Bible
- We believe that the Bible is God's Word.
- We believe that the Bible is the primary authority for our faith and practice.
- We believe that Christians need to know and study the Old Testament and the New Testament (the Hebrew Scriptures and the Christian Scriptures).

Talking About God

You may have heard words used to describe God, Jesus, or the Holy Spirit. The Scriptures contain many words and phrases that people used to name or describe the fullness of God's nature, Christ's identity, or the Spirit's work. The most common Hebrew name for God was *Yahweh*. Jesus called God Abba, which can be translated Daddy. In the gospels, Jesus is called Teacher, the Good Shepherd, and Lord. The Holy Spirit is referred to as the Comforter and the Advocate. Think about which of these words and phrases hold the most meaning for you. How have the words and phrases you use to describe God changed over the years? To what do you attribute the changes? Write your thoughts in the space on the next page.

How Do We Know
What Our Theology Is?

Our theology is shaped by the Bible, by our Christian traditions, by our experiences, and by how we interpret these things. The hymns we sing, the prayers we utter, the rituals we participate in, and the creeds we profess are some of the ways we express our understanding of the Christian faith. We are surrounded by words and symbols that are our attempt to name the reality of God's love and grace in our lives. Our context influences how we interpret faith language, rituals, symbols, and practices. The particularities of who we are affect the value and degree of importance we assign to these practices.

Reading Scripture

What is your favorite Bible story or passage? What does it say about God, about Jesus, about the church?

How long has this story been your favorite? Are there particular circumstances that bring it to mind? How have you called upon the story to remind you of your faith, to find comfort, or to seek guidance? Write your thoughts in the space below.

The Bible, of course, is a book about God and God's relationship with human beings. As United Methodist Christians we believe that Scripture is our primary source for faith and practice. The Bible bears witness to the reality of God in our midst.

Genesis 1:1 begins the story of God's self-revelation with the words, "In the beginning when God created the heavens and the earth . . ." The story continues in verses 26 and 27: "Then God said, 'Let us make humankind in our image, according to our likeness'; . . . in the image of God he created them; male and female he created them." This ancient narrative of our origins concludes with the awesome testimony: "God saw everything that he had made, and indeed, it was very good" (1:31). As a Christian people we proclaim that before there was anything, there was God. The essence of God's nature is creative and relational. We have been created in God's image. What God has created is good.

The rest of the Bible recounts how often human beings failed to live up to God's image within them; how often they worshiped success, wealth, or power instead of worshiping God; and how often they devalued, oppressed, and killed one another. The Scriptures also witness to God's steadfast love and forgiveness. Again and again God reestablishes God's relationship with humanity. Again and again God shows the way to union—or reunion—with God. This witness is most evident in Jesus Christ, who came that we might be reunited with God.

In the church we use the word *sin* for actions and attitudes that separate us from God and God's will. We use the word *grace* for God's generosity and unconditional love toward us. And we use the words *reconciliation* and *salvation* for God's action in Jesus Christ. These concepts are basic to the Christian story. Indeed, the story of the church, including today's church, is the ongoing story of God's reconciling work through Jesus Christ.

Paying Attention to Jesus

In order to know what God is like, we can pay attention to the life, ministry, and death of Jesus.

Take a look at the eighth chapter of Mark's Gospel (the Book of Mark). In many ways this chapter is a microcosm of Jesus' ministry. The chapter begins with Jesus feeding four thousand people. It continues with Jesus healing a blind man. Then Jesus has a conversation with his disciples about what people are saying about him, and Peter professes his faith that Jesus is God's chosen Messiah. The chapter concludes with Jesus calling the disciples to "deny themselves and take up their cross and follow me" (verse 34).

Feeding, healing, teaching, calling—these are the essential elements of Jesus' ministry. If we agree that we can know God through Jesus, then these actions provide clues to who God is and what God wants from us. God cares about our physical needs as well as our spiritual needs. God provides for our needs. God wants us to live as Jesus did, not focusing on our own needs but trusting that God will provide all we need, and living a life of service to the world in the name of Jesus.

Praising God Through Singing

Think back to the earliest song you remember singing in Sunday school or church. What was the song? What words did it use to describe God? What clues to the Christian life did it hold?

I remember singing a song that went something like, "God is love. Praise God, praise God. All God's children praise. God is love." The next verses said, "Love God, love God," and "Serve God, serve God." What a wonderful foundation for theology! From the time I was a small child, I was taught that God is a God of love first and foremost. And what, according to the song, should be my response to God's abundant love? How could it be anything else but praise, love, and joyful service?

Our worship life is rich with hymns and songs that express our faith in God through Christ. Whether we are singing an old hymn, such as "This Is My Father's World," or a contemporary praise song, such as "Lord, I Lift Your Name on High," the words express our understanding of who God is, what God has done for us, and how we choose to respond.

Participating in the Church's Common Life

Consider a typical Sunday in your congregation. More than likely, there are practices that happen each week. These practices may include

- lighting candles on the altar;
- greeting one another and offering the peace of Christ to one another;
- sharing prayer concerns with the congregation.

Now think about a typical month in your congregation. More than likely, the congregation will observe one or more of the following traditions:

- celebrating Holy Communion;
- baptizing a child or adult;
- extending the "hand of fellowship" to a family who desires to take the vows of church membership.

Each of these occasions is marked with familiar words and actions, called rituals. From a practical standpoint, rituals help us know what to do because we've done them before. From a theological standpoint, rituals express our faith. Lighting candles reminds us that Jesus is the light of the world. Sharing prayer concerns reminds us that we are the body of Christ, and if any member of the body suffers, we all suffer (1 Corinthians 12:26). Gathering around the Lord's Table for Holy Communion reminds us what God has done for us through Jesus Christ, and that Christ is present with us through the sacrament.

What you believe about God has been shaped by the practices of the congregations you have been a part of.

Since most of the practices are not explained during a worship service, their purpose is most likely understood implicitly. As a teacher, part of your responsibility is to reflect on these practices, to bring their significance to a conscious level, and to provide space and opportunity for your group members to do the same.

Look at one of the worship bulletins from your congregation. In what ways were you invited to pray? Which of the above rituals were included in the service? What images and actions of God were celebrated? How did any of these practices help you connect with God during worship? Write your thoughts in the space below.

Affirming Our Faith

Throughout the centuries as people discussed and debated matters of faith, various church councils created written statements of belief. These statements, or creeds, provided a concise record of mainstream theology of the time.

Perhaps the most familiar creed today is the Apostles' Creed. This creed was based on similar statements of faith used in baptism rituals as early as the second century. The current form of this creed was written in the eighth century. Notice how the opening affirmation from this creed reflects the biblical understanding of who God is: "I believe in God the Father Almighty, maker of heaven and earth." The creed continues with affirmations about Jesus, the Holy Spirit, the church, the forgiveness of sins, and eternal life.

You can look in *The United Methodist Hymnal* or *The United Methodist Book of Worship* and find several creeds written in more recent times. Sometimes confirmation classes write an affirmation of their faith that is then used in the worship service during which they are confirmed.

The importance of such written statements of faith grows out of the thought and prayer that goes into their formation. At their best they represent our ongoing dialogue about the reality of God. They are not static definitions but dynamic thought processes taking shape in our midst and encouraging us to join the dialogue.

The Apostles' Creed

I believe in God the Father Almighty,
   maker of heaven and earth;

And in Jesus Christ his only Son our Lord:
   who was conceived by the Holy Spirit,
      born of the Virgin Mary,
      suffered under Pontius Pilate,
      was crucified, dead, and buried;
   the third day he rose from the dead;
   he ascended into heaven,
      and sitteth at the right hand of God the Father
         Almighty;
   from thence he shall come to judge the quick and
      the dead.

I believe in the Holy Spirit,
   the holy catholic* church,
   the communion of saints,
   the forgiveness of sins,
   the resurrection of the body,
   and the life everlasting. Amen.

* *catholic* meaning universal

Reprinted from *The United Methodist Hymnal*, ©
1989 The United Methodist Publishing House; 881.

Understanding Our Context

Each of us is born into a particular family, community, nation, and culture. These units of society include values, customs, priorities, standards, and expectations. As we grow up, we discover what is appropriate and what is inappropriate in our family, congregation, community, and culture. We learn the "rules" for success, as well as the boundaries that we should not ignore.

In addition to these overarching societal factors, there are additional variables that define our context. Some of these are

- gender
- education
- income
- race/ethnicity
- location (rural, suburban, urban)

We can continue to focus the description of our context. Individuals may live alone or may live with a spouse, children, a friend, or other relatives. A family may be living temporarily in a country in which they were not born. A person living alone may have always been single or may be divorced or widowed.

Our cultural context and our personal experiences shape how we view the world. They also shape our theology. We need to understand our context in order to understand the values we hold dear, the assumptions out of which we operate, and the factors that most often influence our decisions and our behavior.

Consider your community and congregation. What factors most significantly influence life in your community? in your congregation? What are the unspoken rules in your congregation? How would you define the core values of your congregation? How does your congregation address community issues? Write your thoughts in the space below.

A Theology of Grace

Our United Methodist heritage is rooted in a deep and profound understanding of God's grace. This incredible grace flows from God's great love for us. Did you have to memorize John 3:16 in Sunday school when you were a child? There was a good reason. This one verse summarizes the gospel: "For God so loved the world that he gave his only Son, so that everyone who believes in him may not perish but may have eternal life." The ability to call to mind God's love and God's gift of Jesus Christ is a rich resource for theology and faith.

Grace can be defined as the love and mercy given to us by God because God wants us to have it, not because of anything we have done to earn it. We read in the Letter to the Ephesians: "For by grace you have been saved through faith, and this is not your own doing; it is the gift of God—not the result of works, so that no one may boast" (Ephesians 2:8-9).

Think about a time when you have experienced God's love and grace in your life. Describe that time in the space below.

John Wesley, the founder of the Methodist movement, described God's grace as threefold:
- prevenient grace
- justifying grace
- sanctifying grace

Prevenient Grace

Wesley understood grace as God's active presence in our lives. This presence is not dependent on human actions or human response. It is a gift—a gift that is always available, but that can be refused.

God's grace stirs up within us a desire to know God and empowers us to respond to God's invitation to be in relationship with God. God's grace enables us to discern differences between good and evil and makes it possible for us to choose good.

What captures my attention in this dimension of God's grace is the initiative that God takes in relating to humanity. We do not have to beg and plead for God's love and grace. God actively seeks us!

Justifying Grace

Paul wrote to the church in Corinth: "In Christ God was reconciling the world to himself, not counting their trespasses against them" (2 Corinthians 5:19). And in his letter to the Roman Christians, Paul wrote: "But God proves his love for us in that while we still were sinners Christ died for us" (Romans 5:8).

These verses demonstrate the justifying grace of God. They point to reconciliation, pardon, and restoration. Through the work of God in Christ our sins are forgiven, and our relationship with God is restored. According to John Wesley, founder of the Methodist movement, the image of God—which has been distorted by sin—is renewed within us through Christ's death.

Again, this dimension of God's grace is a gift. God's grace alone brings us into relationship with God. There are no hoops through which we have to jump in order to please God and to be loved by God. God has acted in Jesus Christ. We need only to respond in faith.

Sanctifying Grace

Salvation is not a static, one-time event in our lives. It is the ongoing experience of God's gracious presence transforming us into whom God intends us to be. John Wesley described this dimension of God's grace as sanctification, or holiness.

Through God's sanctifying grace we grow and mature in our ability to live as Jesus lived. As we pray, study the Scriptures, fast, worship, and share in fellowship with other Christians, we deepen our knowledge of and love for God. As we respond with compassion to human need and work for justice in our communities, we strengthen our capacity to love neighbor. Our inner thoughts and motives, as well as our outer actions and behavior, are aligned with God's will and testify to our union with God.

Think about the group you lead. In what ways does your teaching help group members experience God's grace? What evidence do you see that they are growing and maturing in their faith? Write your thoughts in the space below.

A Theology
of Discipleship

Theology is not just about God. It is also about us. We live out of our understanding of who we are in relationship to God, to one another, and to the world. The Christian faith is grounded in the love and grace of God, experienced through Jesus Christ, and empowered by the Holy Spirit. The Christian life is our response to God's love and grace.

The church calls our response to God *Christian discipleship*. Discipleship focuses on actively following in the footsteps of Jesus. As Christian disciples, we are not passive spectators but energetic participants in God's activity in the world. Because of what God has done for us, we offer our lives back to God. We order our lives in ways that embody Christ's ministry in our families, workplaces, communities, and the world.

Loving God

When Jesus was asked what the most important commandment was, his response was: "'You shall love the Lord your God with all your heart, and with all your soul, and with all your mind.' This is the greatest and first commandment" (Matthew 22:37-38. See Matthew 22:34-40; Mark 12:28-34; and Luke 10:25-28.)

Discipleship is about loving God. Let me say that again. Discipleship is about loving God. It is more than an acknowledgment of God's existence or a statement of belief regarding God. It is total devotion, head-over-heels-in-love-with adoration. It is the deep desire to know God, to be one with God, and to worship God.

There are a variety of ways that we can develop our knowledge of and love for God. These include

- prayer
- Bible study
- worship
- fasting
- conversation with other Christians

John Wesley, founder of the Methodist movement, called these practices means of grace. They are means for developing our relationship with God and for experiencing God's presence in our lives. These practices help us spend time with God, a significant factor in loving God.

Loving Neighbor

Jesus responded to questions about the most important commandment by quoting the Hebrew Scripture's admonition to love God with our whole being. (See Deuteronomy 6:4-9 as well as the gospel passages listed in the above section.) Then immediately he broadened the meaning of this admonition: "The second is this, 'You shall love your neighbor as yourself'" (Mark 12:31).

These verses about loving God and loving neighbor as ourselves are known as the Great Commandment. Again and again the Bible teaches us that loving God and loving neighbor are two sides of the same coin. We cannot do one without the other. Check out some of these passages for a glimpse at how prevalent this understanding of Christian discipleship is:

- Matthew 5:43-48
- Matthew 25:31-46
- Luke 10:25-37
- John 15:12-17
- Romans 12:9-18
- 1 Corinthians 13
- 1 John 4:19-21

From these passages and others we can draw several conclusions about what it means to love our neighbors. First of all, loving our neighbors means responding to specific needs—hunger, illness, imprisonment, loneliness, and so forth. Love is more than a feeling; it is behavior. It is practical and concrete.

Secondly, our neighbors include many people. Within the context of the Christian community, our neighbors are our brothers and sisters in Christ. Neighbors may also refer to the contemporary understanding of those who live near us. However, from a biblical perspective, neighbors often include people whom we might not normally consider:

- strangers;
- prisoners;
- people who mistreat us (who are our enemies);
- people from other cultural and ethnic backgrounds;
- people from different religious traditions;
- people who irritate us and push the boundaries of our patience.

Therefore, loving our neighbors requires attention and sacrifice. We have to pay attention to what is happening around us in order to see our neighbors and to recognize their needs. We must also consider their needs to be as important as our own in order to live faithfully. Loving neighbor is more than random acts of kindness. It takes time, energy, and commitment. It is a lifestyle carefully cultivated in response to God.

Finally, these passages emphasize that loving our neighbors is not optional; it is mandatory. It is what Christians do and who Christians are. Our lives are a testimony to our love—our love for God and our love for neighbor.

Reflect on how you plan learning experiences for your group. In what ways do these experiences cultivate loving God and loving neighbor? In what ways do you need to deepen these experiences? Write your thoughts in the space below.

Making Disciples

The last verses of the Gospel of Matthew are known as the Great Commission. They read: "Go therefore and make disciples of all nations, baptizing them in the name of the Father and of the Son and of the Holy Spirit, and teaching them to obey everything that I have commanded you. And remember, I am with you always, to the end of the age" (Matthew 28:19-20).

These words are significant for the church's understanding of its mission. In this last conversation Jesus has with his disciples, he sends them into the world to share the good news of God's love and grace. He calls them to the ministry of proclamation, teaching, baptism, and obedience. He describes their ministry as making disciples.

Back up a few verses to find where and when this conversation takes place. The resurrected Christ meets the eleven disciples on a mountain in Galilee. (At this point Judas Iscariot has hanged himself.) Now look at Matthew 5, which is one of the earliest accounts that Matthew gives of Jesus' ministry. In this passage, known as the Sermon on the Mount, where do we find Jesus? There he is—up on a mountain. And what is he talking about? You guessed it—discipleship! Jesus speaks to the crowd: "You are the light of the world. A city built on a hill cannot be hid. No one after lighting a lamp puts it under the bushel basket, but on the lampstand, and it gives light to all in the house. In the same way, let your light shine before others, so that they may see your good works and give glory to your Father in heaven" (Matthew 5:14-16).

Jesus is on a mountaintop teaching about discipleship—about loving God and loving neighbor—at the beginning of his ministry and at the end of his earthly life and ministry. Matthew frames the life and ministry of Jesus with these stories to emphasize his theological understanding about who Jesus is.

Think for a moment about who else in the Bible went up a mountain and came back down with a word from the Lord. (I'll give you a hint: Look in Exodus 19 and 20.) Moses met God on Mount Sinai after leading the Hebrews out of slavery in Egypt in obedience to God's command. There in the wilderness God gave the Ten Commandments to the Israelites through God's spokesperson, Moses. These commands became the centerpiece of the Jewish law that defined God's covenant relationship with the people.

Matthew's Gospel implicitly establishes a parallel between Moses and Jesus as prophets and spokespersons for God. Just as the Hebrews of long ago believed that God acted through Moses to free them from slavery and teach them about life in relationship with God, so we believe that God acted through Jesus to free us from the slavery of sin and death and teach us about life in relationship with God. That life, for Christians, is based not on conformity to rules and regulations but on the love and grace of God through Jesus Christ. Discipleship is our response to this great gift.

Read the following Scriptures and reflect upon what they mean for your personal discipleship: Matthew 5:43-48; Matthew 25:31-46; Luke 10:25-37; John 15:12-17; Romans 12:9-18; 1 Corinthians 13; 1 John 4:19-21. Write your reflections in the space below.

Theology and Teaching

The Christian community is a teaching and learning community. Our learning is lifelong and ongoing. Together we develop knowledge and skills. Together we experience God's presence and the fellowship of Christian community. Together we learn to listen to God. We discover God's call to us as individuals and as members of the faith community. Together we discern meaning and purpose for our lives.

As a teacher, you have the extraordinary opportunity to provide settings for these experiences to occur. You can lead your group members as they study together, serve in the community, and reflect on what they are learning. You can develop your ability to ask questions, value differences of opinion, and encourage inquiry and exploration. You can help class members examine their values, identify sources of authority, and test their assumptions. You can learn to listen to the hunger for truth in the people of faith you have been called to teach.

How you take advantage of this opportunity will be theology in action. And remember, as you respond to this call, you will be following in the footsteps of Jesus, who was also called Teacher and who promised to be with us always, to the end of the age.

Think about a recent experience you had in your class, such as a class service project or a new member joining the class. Are there particular Scriptures that come to mind that relate to this experience? How did the class's understanding of God influence their actions? What questions could you raise that would help the class reflect upon the theological significance of this experience? Write your reflections in the space below.

Going Further

As you read this booklet, you may have identified an interest in or need for further learning. Here are some ideas that you may want to explore:

- Enroll in *Disciple* Bible study, a 34-week comprehensive study of the Bible.
- Enroll in *Christian Believer*, a 34-week comprehensive study of Christian doctrine.
- Participate in a small group that reads Scripture and prays together.
- Read "Our Theological Task" in *The Book of Discipline of The United Methodist Church*.
- View *Legacy of Faith*, a video that documents the contributions of African Americans in our denomination and demonstrates how changing theological perspectives affected the African American members of our church.

- Review the curriculum resources you are using with your class. Make note of the words and images used to describe God, Jesus, the Holy Spirit, human beings, the church, and the Bible. Consider how these words and images reinforce or challenge your own ideas of God.
- Read *Keeping in Touch: Christian Formation and Teaching,* by Carol F. Krau. Pay particular attention to Chapter 4, "Keeping in Touch With Your Experience." Discuss the questions at the end of the chapter with another teacher or small-group leader.
- Use the Internet to explore contemporary church issues and to find resources for your teaching. (See "Helpful Resources," page 47, for ideas.)

Helpful Resources

Websites

General Board of Discipleship of The United Methodist Church (www.gbod.org). On this site you will find articles related to discipleship and teaching. Particular sites of interest are www.gbod.org/education and www.gbod.org/keepingintouch.

Discipleship Resources (www.discipleshipresources.org). In this online bookstore you can purchase additional copies of this booklet, other booklets in the series, and other books published by Discipleship Resources.

The United Methodist Church (www.umc.org). On this site you can find news articles related to the United Methodist denomination, as well as official church responses to current events. You can also locate your annual conference's web page and find out what's happening in your area.

Books

Accountable Discipleship: Living in God's Household, by Steven W. Manskar (Discipleship Resources, 2000). Describes some of the unique emphases of Wesleyan theology.

Keeping in Touch: Christian Formation and Teaching, by Carol F. Krau (Discipleship Resources, 1999). Examines key processes needed by teachers.

Sacraments & Discipleship: Understanding Baptism and the Lord's Supper in a United Methodist Context, by Mark W. Stamm (Discipleship Resources, 2001). Discusses the United Methodist understanding of the sacraments in relation to discipleship.

10 FAQ's of New Christians, by Peter Harrington (Discipleship Resources, 2000). Simple explanation of basic Christian beliefs. Designed for people new to the Christian faith.

Ordering Information

Resources published by Discipleship Resources may be ordered online at www.discipleshipresources.org; by phone at 800-685-4370; by fax at 770-442-9742; or by mail from Discipleship Resources Distribution Center, P.O. Box 1616, Alpharetta, GA 30009-1616.